THE
SECOND
JUMBO BOOK
OF
HIDDEN PICTURES

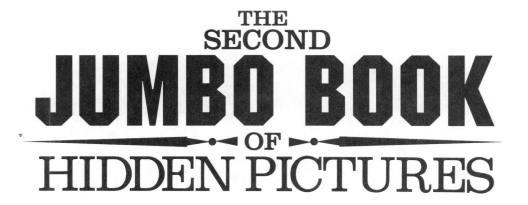

MORE THAN **1000** OBJECTS TO FIND!

Compiled by the Editors of
Highlights for Children

BOYDS MILLS PRESS

Cover
Home Sweet Home

The cat's out of harm's way, so the mice are having a feast. While they munch away, try to find a seal, cane, number 2, snail, bird, banana, rabbit, fish, and a crescent moon.

Copyright © 1993 by Boyds Mills Press

Boyds Mills Press, Inc.
A Highlights Company
815 Church Street
Honesdale, Pennsylvania 18431
Printed in the United States of America

Publisher Cataloging-in-Publication Data
The second jumbo book of hidden pictures / compiled by the
editors of Highlights for Children.
[96]p. : ill. ; cm.
Summary: Each illustrated page presents a challenge to find various
hidden objects.
ISBN 1-56397-185-2
1. Puzzles—Juvenile literature. [1. Picture puzzles.]
I. Highlights for Children. II. Title.
793.73—dc20   1993
Library of Congress Catalog Card Number 92-71869

First edition, 1993
The text of this book is set in 10-point Clarendon Light.

20 19 18 17 16 15

The Basketball Game

Basketball games are always challenging, but finding these hidden objects is, too. Can you find a pea pod, sewing needle, chicken, cat, pitcher, iron, football, spool of thread, flower pot, bowling pin, saltshaker, sea gull, bottle, ladle, acorn, and a harmonica?

Snowtime Fun

Building a snowman is lots of fun, but so is looking for hidden objects. Can you help the children uncover these hidden objects: a comb, toothbrush, Abe Lincoln, canoe, key, pie, candle, flashlight, shoe, sailboat, gavel, spoon, frying pan, boot, carrot, and an umbrella?

4

Lemonade Stand

Leah opened a lemonade stand in the shade of the oak trees. Little did she know there were many hidden objects in this shady spot. Can you point out the hidden objects to Leah? There is a broom, worm, pig, fish, horse, cat, frog, screwdriver, mouse, duck, lobster, daffodil, ostrich, and a gorilla's profile in this picture.

Wake Up, It's Spring!

The mice and elves are waking up to celebrate spring. Can you help them find these objects that were stored until spring: a canoe, birdhouse, safety pin, dog, bird, umbrella, spoon, duck, glove, heart, sailboat, horse's head, telescope, and a cupcake?

Gone Fishing

On a hot summer day Katie Joe loves to imagine she's gone fishing. Can you help her reel in these hidden objects: a bird, bell, artist's paintbrush, pencil, snake, trowel, hat, shark, frying pan, snail, high-heeled shoe, dog's head, carrot, and a fish?

Springtime Cleanup

The mice are working very hard to clean up Captain Jack's house today. Perhaps they will be able to locate these misplaced objects: a bird, umbrella, bow tie, doll, glove, telephone receiver, rabbit, dog, paper boat, ladle, bubble pipe, and a bunch of bananas.

Painting a Dollhouse

The children are giving a coat of paint to a newly built dollhouse. Hidden in this picture are these objects: a closed book, two birds, hen, rooster, apple, bow, wrench, spoon, open book, teacup, car, anchor, shark, and a comb.

Carousel Ride

Round and round the carousel goes, taking its riders on a joyous trip. On the way, the children found these hidden objects: a shovel, two spoons, banana, seal, shoe, sewing needle, dinosaur, cowboy hat, sailboat, snail, two ducks, pliers, apple, clothespin, pail, fish, bird, cockatoo, flower in a pot, dolphin, and an ear of corn.

11

Hide 'n' Seek

Bobby is counting to ten while his friends hide in the back yard. In the meantime, can you find the objects hidden in this picture? Find the book, seal, ice-cream cone, crayon, carrot, ring, nail, flashlight, screwdriver, pitcher, fish, teacup, butterfly, scissors, mitten, bird, alligator, and the covered pot.

12

The Toy Maker

Mama Duck is putting the finishing touches on her stuffed monkey. In the picture you will find a boy's profile, mitten, sock, leaf, slice of pie, musical note, elephant, alligator, ring, heart, mushroom, flower, spoon, whale, and a fish.

13

The Zoo

There are lots of animals to see in the zoo. And some of them are cleverly hiding in this picture. Can you find a vulture, python, bear, alligator, hippopotamus, elephant, chimpanzee, leopard, seal, rhinoceros, gorilla, lion, kangaroo, and a giraffe?

Flamingos

Four flamingos prance in the pond, admiring their plumage and unaware of the hidden objects around them. See if you can find a hat, stocking cap, apple, pair of oars, horn, rabbit, hammer, elephant's head, sewing needle, pencil, fish, shoe, pliers, and a screwdriver.

Who's Got the Ball?

The professional football players are battling for possession of the ball, but young Christopher scores the touchdown to end the game. Help him find the slice of pie, envelope, doughnut, ice-cream cone, cat, mouse, telephone receiver, banana, mug, hairbrush, ax, lamb, hammer, and the elephant's head.

All in a Day's Work

The elves are busy gathering wood and water to use in their homes. While they do, find these hidden objects: a bird in a nest, sock, salamander, dog's head, rowboat, squirrel, toothbrush, bear, map, top hat, tree, dog, safety pin, bird, girl reading a book, lamb, beaver, and a bird on a ladder.

Ocean View

The ocean floor harbors the octopus and fish of many kinds. Hidden in the seaweed are these objects: a heart, spoon, house, teacup, koala bear's head, sailboat, banana, flower, shoe, pencil, bell, apple, and a car.

The Soccer Game

Mindy shows some fancy footwork and leads her team to victory. You can score big if you can find these hidden objects: a turkey leg, fish, high-heeled shoe, bird, snail, crescent moon, cupcake, pliers, button, ice-cream cone, canteen, nutcracker, flashlight, bedroom slipper, saltshaker, and a ladder.

The Piñata

Carlos has broken the piñata, and trinkets and sweets tumble out. See if you can find the objects hidden among the treats. Find a caterpillar, open book, croissant, file, scissors, hairbrush, sink plunger, hair dryer, flower pot, pelican, blue jay, and a Mountie's hat.

Frosty Fun

The mice have their share of fun in the snow-covered hills. As they ski, see if you can find the ice-cream cone, snowshoe, snowman, cane, cat, rabbit, sled, earmuffs, sleigh, drinking glass, eyeglasses, boot, mitten, elephant's head, stocking cap, and the horse's head.

Biplane Adventure

The biplane soars above fourteen objects hidden in the farmland below. Help the pilot and copilot find the lizard, rooster, sailboat, hammer, snake, mouse, funnel, open book, umbrella, pencil, rabbit, cup, spoon, and the artist's paintbrush.

Fox and Stork

Stork can't wait to dig in to his favorite soup, served up by Fox the waiter. As Stork eats, try to find the baseball cap, fish, cane, duck, ladle, ring, sewing needle, scissors, boot, butterfly, nail, ice-cream cone, and the turtle.

Flat Tire

The Baker family car may have a flat tire, but that doesn't stop the folks from enjoying the scenery, which contains twelve hidden objects: a loaf of bread, ice-cream cone, spoon, funnel, slice of pie, celery stalk, cupcake, jar, pen, crayon, mallet, and an open book.

The Night Heron

The night heron stands guard over the marsh, protecting its nest. Surrounding the bird are thirteen hidden objects: a monkey's head, shark, lizard, chipmunk, rabbit, spoon, rhinoceros's head, pitchfork, cardinal, snake, loon, artist's paintbrush, and a beaver.

Elephant Bath

Baby elephant gets a playful shower from his loving mother. They're having too much fun to notice the hidden objects in this picture. Can you find the airplane, bird, spoon, feather, lamb, cupcake, banana, mushroom, magic lamp, dog, crescent moon, football, duck, trowel, and the safari hat?

Skating Bears

Out of the way! The Bear family is skating down Main Street. They're moving too fast to see the hidden objects. See if you can find the toothbrush, artist's paintbrush, high-heeled shoe, telephone receiver, baseball, spaceship, stopwatch, screwdriver, carrot, spatula, tape dispenser, mushroom, balloon, teacup, orange slice, and the sink plunger.

The Road Race

The horseless carriage has taken the lead in its race with the horse and buggy. As they head for the finish line, see if you can find the carrot, bear's head, bottle, flute, squirrel, worm, snow shovel, egg, metronome, rabbit, teacup, book, measuring compass, banana, and the orange slice.

28

The Farm Family

Farmer Jones and his family pose for a photograph outside their barn. Do they know there are hidden objects surrounding them? Find the duck, drum, slice of pie, paintbrush, nail, banana, carrot, spoon, hammer, eyeglasses, tea kettle, pencil, ice-cream cone, spool of thread, and the bowl.

Hot-Air Balloon Trip

Three adventurous travelers say good-bye to their woodland friends as they embark on a hot-air balloon journey. Hidden around them are fifteen objects: a mushroom, dolphin, iced cake, horse's head, spider, flag, golf club, ice-cream cone, sock, hammer, pail, envelope, roller skate, rolling pin, and a feather. Can you find them?

Star Gazing

Looking through the telescope, the boys and girls can clearly see the moon's craters. Can you find the golf club, straw hat, ladle, pie, spoon, sewing needle, mop, letter **A**, crescent moon, screwdriver, toothbrush, cup, sea gull, ice-cream cone, chef's hat, bird, drinking glass, ladder, and the bell in the picture?

Class Play

Jimmy and Cindy are starring in *Romeo and Juliet,* but that cat doesn't belong there and neither do the hidden objects. Can you find the cup, ladybug, cupcake, turtle, gavel, ice-cream cone, pair of shorts, coat hanger, artist's paintbrush, hammer, broom, stool, fish, and the bowling ball?

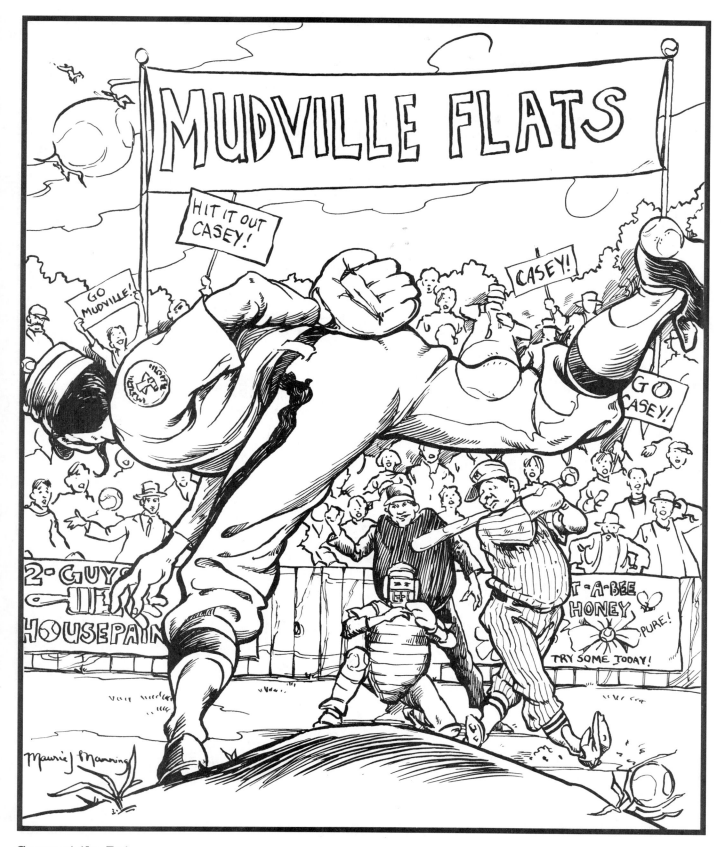

Casey at the Bat

The legendary Casey is taking his turn at the plate. But which ball should he swing at? There are eleven of them in this picture. Can you find them all?

Planting a Tree

The neighborhood kids are helping the environment by planting a tree in the park. As they dig, find the owl, gopher, parrot, frog, glove, clippers, ladle, butterfly, rabbit, arrowhead, squirrel, snail, ladder, pitchfork, slice of pie, fox, fish, and the duck.

Midnight Snack

Bear's raiding the refrigerator for a nighttime feast. His kitchen is full of hidden objects. Help him find a toothbrush, ice-cream cone, open book, flashlight, banana, orange slice, pencil, knife, spoon, mallet, flower, party hat, mushroom, and a wristwatch.

The Swiss Elves

The Swiss elves are skating and skiing over the snow-capped mushrooms. Hidden in their mountain retreat are a flower, magician, camel, ice-cream sundae, ear of corn, sailboat, sock, parrot's head, dog, sombrero, woman, teacup, elephant's head, brush, boot, elf, and a boy.

The Blacksmith's Shop

The blacksmith has more in his shop than meets the eye. Can you find the sewing needle, motorcycle helmet, mailbox, arrowhead, pencil, funnel, perfume bottle, boot, rocking horse, spray gun, pig's head, elephant's head, and the sandpiper?

Sandbox Fun

While the boys and girls build a construction site in the sandbox, you can find a butterfly, carrot, fish, teacup, whistle, crayon, seal, paper clip, wide-brimmed hat, ladybug, safety pin, camera, sandpiper, sailboat, and an ear of corn.

Picnic Paradise

The ants have found the food. But can they find the dragonfly, trowel, flag, sewing needle, coat hanger, fly, artist's paintbrush, book, hammer, mouse, arrow, pear, pencil, sailboat, and the number 7 hidden in the picture?

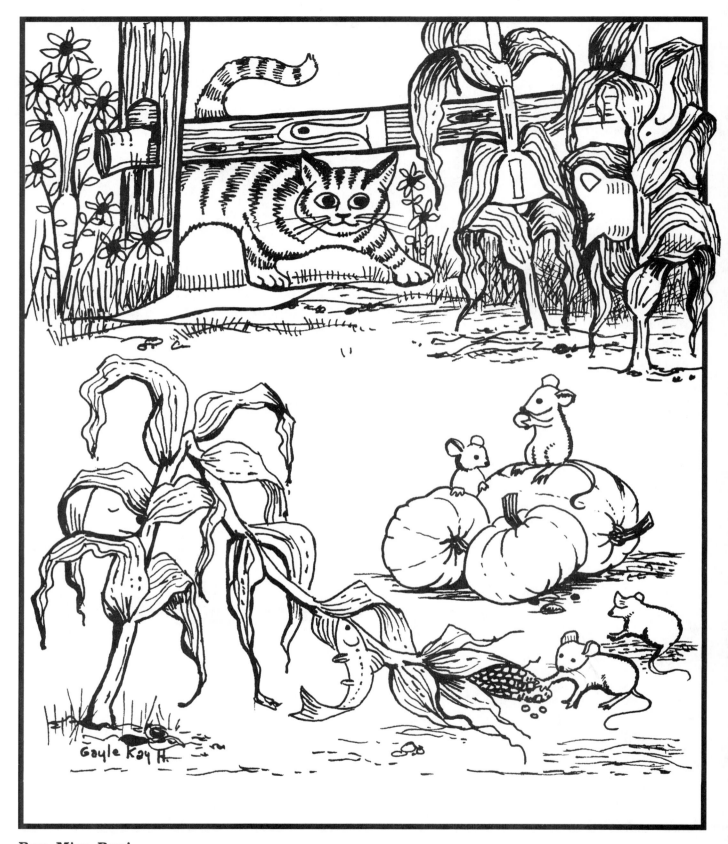

Run, Mice, Run!

Can the mice see that they're in danger? And can you see the hidden objects? Try to find a wide-brimmed hat, boot, carrot, bell, pitcher, bird, fish, paintbrush, and a dog's head.

Aztec Marketplace

Hidden among the goods for sale are seventeen objects, including a shoe, sewing needle, crescent moon, toothbrush, hummingbird, lizard, milk carton, butterfly, snail, snake, dragonfly, bird, pencil, insect, ear of corn, rabbit, and a fish. How many can you find?

Puppet Show

Heather and Philip entertain their friends with a puppet show. As they watch, try to find a necktie, rabbit, comb, book, turtle, wishbone, carrot, teacup, penguin, broom, acorn, cat, fish, snail, and a toothbrush.

Piglets Take a Holiday

Boating and fishing are very popular activities at the Siloville Hotel. While the piglets enjoy the outdoors, look for the pair of shorts, doll, bird, fish, flag, elephant, duck, sea gull, basket, bowl, open book, golf club, woman, party hat, shoe, baseball bat, walkie-talkie, and the boy with the hat.

Pignic

The three pigs munch on one of their favorite foods—corn. Surrounding them are twelve hidden objects. See if you can find a lock, shovel, saltshaker, toothbrush, cupcake, feather duster, slice of cake with a candle on top, hairbrush, tube of paint, teacup, banana, and a radish.

Mr. and Mrs. Jack Sprat

The Sprats are on a fat-free diet, but somehow Mrs. Sprat manages to stay plump. As they drink their tea, find the doll, fish, two birds, basket, squirrel, bell, cat, and the dog.

Circus Elephant

Hidden within the circus grounds are twelve objects: a pair of pants, hammer, coffee pot, turtle, two fish, fork, bird, vase, owl, face, and a pig's head. Can you find them?

Deena's Diner

The frogs know that Deena serves the best fly soup in the pond. Try to find a bird, ice-cream cone, bell, race car, paintbrush, mitten, sock, cat, slipper, elephant's head, crayon, toothbrush, screwdriver, fish, shovel, slice of pie, golf club, boot, and a wishbone as they eat lunch.

Sea Dogs

The canine crew keeps the boat shipshape as the sea dogs sail the seas. Can you help them find the hidden objects? Look for a coat hanger, bird, number 9, duck, screwdriver, mushroom, paper clip, candle, ice-cream pop, bell, artist's paintbrush, heart, fish, and a kangaroo.

Ben Franklin's Experiment

The great inventor places a key on his kite's tail, waiting for lightning to strike. In the meantime, try to find the airplane, clothespin, spoon, dinosaur, carrot, rabbit, ice-cream cone, sailboat, light bulb, fish, bird, cup, mouse, banana, paper clip, squirrel, and the toothbrush.

Hiking

The children are on the trail of the hidden objects. Help them find a carrot, cupcake, mug, candle, toothbrush, frying pan, flashlight, wristwatch, spoon, apple, eyeglasses, key, and a safety pin.

The New House

The mice have a new home. They're too busy to find the hidden objects. In this picture look for a spaceship, shoe, elf's face, star, vase, fish, heart, owl, carrot, baseball cap, pliers, weasel, peanut, and a butterfly.

The Deer

The deer are wary of the strange sounds they hear in the woods. They can't see the hidden objects there. Can you? Look for a lamb's head, mouse, fish, cat, seal, snake, pie, bee, dog, and a lizard.

Horseshoes

Daniel pitched a ringer. It's fun playing horseshoes. And it's fun finding these hidden objects: a fish, iron, bell, mouse, duck, ice-cream cone, eyeglasses, top, artist's paintbrush, bedroom slipper, baseball bat, chicken, canoe, whistle, and a safety pin.

Construction Site

The construction workers are building around the hidden objects. Can you find a bicycle pump, crayon, snow shovel, bunch of grapes, screwdriver, funnel, briefcase, chair, owl, flower pot, half of an apple, artist's paintbrush, slice of cake with a candle on top, magnifying glass, ice-cream pop, sneaker, clothes hanger, canoe, flashlight, open book, safety pin, slice of pie, witch's hat, telephone, cowboy hat, and a flower?

55

Snowman

The children stand back and admire the snowman they created. Within the scene are ten objects. Find a sailboat, bird, ax, teacup, comb, teapot, banana, snake, bowl, and a pencil.

Dragon's Game

The dragon challenges Andy to find the hidden objects. See if you can spot the hammer, football, teacup, pencil, apple, ring, scissors, pitcher, duck, spool of thread, fish, bottle, and the ice-cream cone.

The Baker

Grandma makes the best chocolate chip cookies, say Maggie and Henry. Her recipe for fun calls for finding hidden objects. Look for a teacup, slice of pie, artist's paintbrush, saltshaker, spoon, slice of pizza, fish, crown, cane, hammer, wishbone, whistle, pencil, pancake flipper, ice-cream cone, toothbrush, and a wristwatch.

Scarecrow

The scarecrow can't seem to keep the hidden objects away. Find the turtle, rabbit, two birds, bell, worm, ring, bee, butterfly, rake, bunch of grapes, watering can, rooster, pitchfork, and the hoe.

The Knight

Riding on horseback, the knight seeks the hidden objects in the forest. Help him find the snake, spaceship, skate, comb, cane, two goldfish, candle, shovel, horseshoe, telephone receiver, ice-cream cone, scissors, octopus, whale, rabbit, sailboat, pumpkin, teacup, plum, lizard, bird, pig, and a cookie.

Kids in the Kitchen

Everyone's busy in the kitchen, even the cats. Find the safety pin, handbag, sailboat, duck, button, pencil, hat, and the fish in this picture.

Three for Tea

Three fairies rest and drink tea at their mushroom table. In this scene try to find a bird, cowboy, rocking horse, rooster's head, ballerina, fish, sock, pig, and a trowel.

Westward Wagon

The Johnson family heads west to a new farm in Iowa. On the way find these hidden objects: a teacup, old woman's profile, two birds, open book, boot, lunch box, boomerang, thimble, telephone receiver, mushroom, funnel, snail, nail, scissors, bow tie, and a fish.

Hungry Raccoons

The Raccoon family has found a meal for the day. You can find the following hidden pictures: a heart, worm, ladybug, baseball bat, banana, mug, nail, turtle, pencil, two cherries, and a fish.

64

Wake-Up Time

Scruffy awakens Jennifer, who's ready to start the day. In this picture find a seal, banana, crescent moon, bird, ladder, candle, spoon, rabbit, mop, golf club, feather, duck, shoe, fish, flying sea gull, and a mouse.

Riverboat

As the paddle-wheel boat chugs down the Mississippi, find the spool of thread, wedge of cheese, bottle, dog, saw, comb, orange slice, ladder, bird, banjo, toothbrush, fish, and the cooking pot.

The Frog and the Princess

The princess wishes to find the hidden objects in this picture. Help her look for a mouse, fork, glove, bear, chicken, rabbit, sled, open book, sheep, high-heeled shoe, cat, bird, turtle, and a fish.

Piggy Goes to Market

The ducks and chickens scatter as Piggy heads to the market. During his trip he finds a comb, slice of pie, acorn, pliers, hammer, ice-cream cone, shoe, baseball cap, rowboat, cup, paintbrush, and a whale. Can you find them all?

Camping Out

Mom and Dad pitch the tent as the kids get ready to sleep under the stars. Hidden around the campsite are seventeen objects: a wishbone, toothbrush, rowboat, candy dish, carrot, lizard, artist's paintbrush, teacup, slice of pie, ice-cream scoop, snake, trowel, sun visor, pencil, gavel, spoon, and a flashlight. Can you find them?

The Roundup

A lone cowboy readies his lasso to rope a wandering steer. Hidden around the range are fourteen objects. Can you find the horseshoe, rabbit, man's profile, scissors, fish, mushroom, comb, teacup, butterfly, boot, letter **M,** bird, fork, and the turkey?

The Garden

The flower garden is full of hidden objects. Find the umbrella, shuttlecock, mannequin, banana, lamp, fish, button, hummingbird, spoon, hammer, candy cane, tube of toothpaste, and the saltshaker.

Neighborhood Parade

The Wilson Avenue Marching Band struts its stuff for the neighborhood. As the music plays, find the mitten, half of an orange, spool of thread, banana, ruler, fishhook, light bulb, pencil, ladle, swan, saltshaker, eagle's head, dustpan, sunglasses, bowling pin, comb, lemon wedge, domino, dish, wristwatch, bar of soap, penny, ice-cream pop, ice-cream cone, mug, mushroom, feather, envelope, and the carrot.

The Nest

The nest harbors baby birds and hidden objects. See if you can find the mouse, airplane, baseball cap, dog's head, buffalo, candy cane, pliers, lizard, moth, and the dodo bird's head.

Rip Van Winkle

Hidden around Rip and his bowling partners are these hidden objects: a squirrel, seal, fish, elephant's head, antelope's head, lemon, and a rabbit's head.

The Classroom

The students have their assignments for today. Yours is to find these hidden objects: a slice of toast, open box, pencil, fish, pig, loaf of bread, garden hose, wristwatch, minivan, *Tyrannosaurus rex*, house, bell, horse's head, bird, paintbrush, and an elephant's head.

The Stourbridge Lion

The Stourbridge Lion train powers its way down the railroad tracks to the cheers of the crowd. As the engine roars past, try to find the spool of thread, banana, kite, sewing needle, crayon, envelope, book, ladder, sailboat, snake's head, salamander, butterfly, rooster, hatchet, fish bones, and the funnel.

Answers

Front Cover

page 3

page 4

page 5

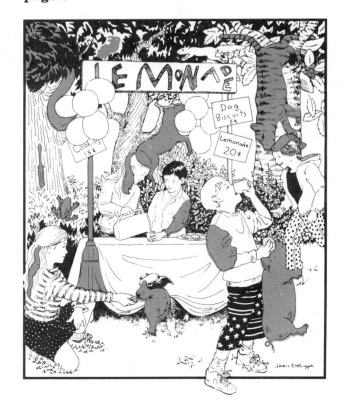

Answers

page 6

page 7

page 8

page 9

Answers

page 10-11

page 12

page 13

Answers

page 14

page 15

page 16

page 17

Answers

page 18

page 19

page 20

page 21

Answers

page 22

page 23

page 24

page 25

Answers

page 26

page 27

page 28

page 29

Answers

page 30

page 31

page 32

page 33

Answers

page 34

page 35

page 36

page 37

Answers

page 38

page 39

page 40

page 41

Answers

page 42

page 43

page 44

page 45

Answers

page 46

page 47

page 48

page 49

Answers

page 50

page 51

page 52

page 53

Answers

page 54-55

page 56

page 57

Answers

page 58

page 59

page 60

page 61

Answers

page 62

page 63

page 64

page 65

Answers

page 66

page 67

page 68

page 69

Answers

page 70

page 71

page 72-73

Answers

page 74

page 75

page 76

page 77